Do Something Beautiful for God

The Essential Teachings of Mother Teresa

BLUE SPARROW
North Palm Beach, Florida

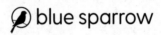

Copyright © 2020
Kakadu, LLC
Published by BLUE SPARROW

All rights reserved.
No part of this book may be used or reproduced in any manner
whatsoever without permission except in the case of brief quotations
in critical articles or reviews.

The quotes in this book have been drawn from dozens of sources.
They are assumed to be accurate as quoted in their previously
published forms. Although every effort has been made to verify the
quotes and sources, the Publisher cannot guarantee their perfect
accuracy.

Design by Ashley Wirfel

ISBN: 978-1-63582-120-8 (hardcover)
ISBN: 978-1-63582-121-5 (e-Book)

10 9 8 7 6 5 4 3 2 1

Printed in the United States of America

Table of Contents

Introduction: Encountering a Saint

IT HAS BEEN twenty years since Mother Teresa died. She died humbly while the whole world was looking the other way. The world was obsessed with the death and funeral of Princess Dianna and Mother Teresa took that opportunity to slip from this world into the arms of her loving God.

Mother Teresa captured the imagination of the whole world—just as the first Christians did—by radically embracing the Gospel message of Jesus.

People from every corner of the world were intrigued with her life and her work. Men, women, and children were fascinated with this Catholic nun in Calcutta. Such is the allusive power of holiness.

She is truly a modern example of how universally attractive holiness is.

Who loved Mother Teresa? Just Catholics? No. Just Christians? No. Mother Teresa was beloved by men and women of all faiths and men and women of no faith. Why? Because there is simply nothing more attractive than holiness. Holiness is irresistible.

Here are just some of the things other people have said about the Saint of Calcutta:

"Mother Teresa marked the history of our century with courage. She served all human beings by promoting their dignity and respect, and made those who had been defeated by life feel the tenderness of God."
—Pope John Paul II

"When she walked into the room to greet me, I felt that I was indeed meeting a saint."
—The Reverend Billy Graham

"Mother Teresa is the United Nations. She is peace in the world."
—Javier Perez de Cuellar, former U.N. Secretary General

"Mother Teresa personified a boldness of spirit and purity of soul revered by the entire world... She served as a model of holiness, virtue, and humility."
—Ronald and Nancy Regan, 40th President of the United States and First Lady

"A loss to the entire humanity. She will be deeply missed in our efforts to build international peace, and a just, caring, and equitable world order."
—Nelson Mandela, former President of South African

"Our world has lost the most celebrated saint of our times. This courageous woman gave hope to millions, and showed us the power of caring and human kindness."
—Coretta Scott King, civil rights leader and widow of Martin Luther King, Jr.

"This evening, there is less love, less compassion, less light in the world. She leaves us a strong message, which has no borders and which goes beyond faith: helping, listening, solidarity."
—Jacques Chirac, French President

But each person who encountered Mother Teresa had his or her own experience. Now it is your turn to encounter her or re-encounter her. Her life and her message are timeless. She reaches deep into our hearts, minds, and souls and challenges us to embrace the beautiful generosity of our own humanity.

Biography: She Captured the Imagination of the Whole World

MOTHER TERESA was born Agnes Bojaxhiu in Serbia on August 26, 1910. Agnes grew up in Albania, surrounded by wealth and prosperity. Despite their wealth, her parents were models of virtue. They loved each other deeply, and that love overflowed to Agnes and her sister. At the age of eighteen, Agnes left home to join an Irish order of nuns. Later that year, in December 1928, she set sail for India to begin her work as a novice for the Loreto Order. Now Sister Teresa, she spent most of the next twenty years teaching. In 1937, she made her permanent vows of poverty, chastity, and obedience, and as was customary adopted the title of Mother.

By 1943, India was torn by war and famine. Mahatma Gandhi's great success in freeing India from British rule had become tainted by civil war between Muslims and Hindus living in India. More people than ever descended upon Calcutta. It finally became necessary for the Loreto Convent to move the children and the school outside the city. At this time, many nuns and whole orders decided to leave India and close their schools, but Mother Teresa stayed and worked tirelessly. As others left, she taught more and more classes, eventually teaching two subjects to eight grades.

She was happy in her work and well liked. By the mid-1940s, her mere presence already had a power that had been born through hours of prayer and reflection. Soon Mother Teresa was appointed headmistress, and she wrote to her mother, "This is a new life. Our center here is very fine. I am a teacher, and I love the work. I am also head of the whole school, and every- body wishes me well." Her mother's reply was a stern reminder of her original intentions for going to India: "Dear child, do not forget that you went to India for the sake of the poor."

Kipling described Calcutta as "the city of a dreadful night." Mother Teresa was in the capital of poverty, a poverty that most people never even witness firsthand, let alone personally experience. Have you been there? Have you seen it on television? Can you picture it?

This was the world that surrounded the school and this was the world that was crying out for help.

In 1946, Mother Teresa became very ill herself and was ordered by doc- tors to have bed rest for three hours every afternoon. It was very hard for her to rest and not do her work, but this period of enforced rest culminated in the directive to go away on retreat for a month. The intention was that in the interests of her health she should undergo a period of spiritual renewal and a physical break from the work.

On September 10, 1946, she boarded a train for Darjeeling, where she was to retreat. Aboard that train, Mother Teresa had a supernatural experience that changed the direction of her life forever. She referred to it as "the call within the call." Many years earlier she had been called to religious life (the call). Now she was being called to something more (the call within the call). The retreat provided the perfect period of silence, solitude, and prayer to follow the experience God had given her on the train.

The next couple of years were filled with dialogue between her spiritual director, the Bishop, and Rome. By 1950, at age forty, Mother Teresa had left the school and the Loreto Order, founded the Sisters of Charity, and was living among the poorest of the poor in Calcutta. At this time she began a new life, dreamt a new dream. She stepped into the classroom of silence, sat down with her God, and said, How can I help? Over the next twenty years she would capture the imagination of the whole world simply by living the Gospel. Such is the potency and spellbinding power the Gospel holds when it is actually lived.

When was the last time you stepped into the classroom of silence, sat down with your God, and asked, How can I help?

Over the next five decades, Mother Teresa emerged as an icon of modern holiness, capturing the imaginations and intriguing the hearts and minds of people from every nation on earth. Dedicated to a life of simplicity, she gave herself to society's most marginalized victims. Her love for people was tangible. You could see it. You could feel it. You could reach out and touch it. It was real and living. It wasn't a sermon or a speech. Each moment, she looked only for the next opportunity to love. For her, every individual mattered. "I believe," she once said, " in person-to-person contact. Every person is Christ for me, and since there is only one Jesus, the person I am meeting is the one person in the world at that moment." Those who spent time with her would often comment, "For the moment you were with her, there was only you and her. She wasn't looking over your shoulder to see what was happening around you. You had her full attention. It was as if nothing else existed to her except you."

Contrasted against the unbridled materialism of the modern world, Mother Teresa had an attraction that seemed impossible to explain. The contrast between the spirit of the world and the spirit of this woman was breathtaking.

Years before, the people of India had traveled hundreds of miles, often on foot, to catch a glimpse of Gandhi. Hindus believe that simply to be in the presence of a holy person brings with it a great blessing. Now they sought the company, the mere presence, even just a glimpse of Mother Teresa, a Catholic nun. Like a magnetic field, she attracted the rich and the poor, the weak and the powerful, irrespective of race or creed.

In time, Mother Teresa was awarded the Nobel Peace Prize, the United States Medal of Freedom, and the United Nations Albert Schweitzer Prize. Considered by many to be a living saint, she didn't allow all the attention to distract her and remained a soul wholly dedicated to a life of service.

Mother Teresa is one of the most beloved women of all time. She was a steadfast voice of love and faith, and yet her power didn't come from the words she used or the awards she received, and she never forced her beliefs upon anyone. Asked to speak about religion, she once said, "Religion is not something that you or I can touch. Religion is the worship of God—therefore a matter of conscience. I alone must decide for myself and you for yourself, what we choose. For me, the religion I live and use to worship God is the Catholic religion. For me, this is my very life, my joy, and the greatest gift of God in his love for me. He could have given me no greater gift."

When I reflect on the life of Mother Teresa the questions I ask myself are: Where does this power to love so deeply come from? Where does the strength to serve so selflessly come from? What is the source of this woman's extraordinary ability to inspire?

The answers to these questions are also deeply embedded in her life. Before everything else, Mother Teresa was a woman of prayer. Each day, she would spend three hours in prayer before the Blessed Sacrament. Her power to love, her strength to endure, and her gift to inspire the masses were all born in the classroom of silence. This woman believed in the centrality of Jesus Christ. She knew his centrality in history and eternity, and she trusted his centrality in her own life. There lies the source: She placed Jesus at the center of her life. In the depths of her heart, she knew that action without prayer was worth nothing.

Mother Teresa's story is remarkable, but the story within the story is equally remarkable. It would be a mistake for us to examine the life of Mother Teresa and not ask some simple questions: How did she learn to live, love, and pray the way she did? Who taught her? Whom did she take as her role model?

These questions lead us to a young Catholic woman Mother Teresa never met, another nun who lived in a Carmelite convent in southern France and died before Mother Teresa was born. Her name was Saint Therese of Lisieux. Therese believed that love is expressed through attention to the small things that fill our daily lives. Mother Teresa practiced "the little way" taught by Therese.

This connection demonstrates that every holy moment is an historic event. Every time we choose to love God and neighbor we change the course of human history, because our holiness echoes in the lives of people in other places and other times.

Therese entered the convent at the age of fifteen and died at age twenty-four, but her influence continues to resonate in the lives of more than forty-five hundred Missionaries of Charity (the order Mother Teresa founded) who work in 133 countries today. It is impossible to measure Saint Therese of Lisieux's impact on history, but it is vast. Each holy moment is deeply personal, but it is also communal and historic. Holiness is not something we do for ourselves; it is something God does in us if we cooperate. And it is something he does in us not for us alone, but for others and for all of history.

Mother Theresa and Therese of Lisieux cooperated with God to create holy moments that had a historic impact. Now God wants to collaborate with you to create holy moments, and who knows how he will use those holy moments to unleash his great love for us all.

Do something beautiful for God is Mother Teresa's enduring invitation to the world. This is not an abstract invitation, but a deeply personal and intimate one. There is so much happening in the world and so much happening within our own hearts, minds, and souls. All this makes it is easy to lose sight of what matters most and get absorbed in what matters least. But in the midst of all this activity and noise, Mother Teresa and all the saints call out to us gently saying: Do something beautiful for God with your life!

January

JANUARY 1

Live simply so others may simply live.

JANUARY 2

Spread love everywhere you go. Let no one ever come to you without leaving happier.

JANUARY 3

There are no great things, only small things with great love. But those small things done with great love become the source of great joy. I don't do great things. I do small things with great love.

JANUARY 4

We need to find God, and He cannot be found in noise and restlessness. God is the friend of silence. See how nature—trees, flowers, grass—grow in silence; see the stars, the moon and the sun, how they move in silence . . . We need silence to be able to touch souls.

JANUARY 5

Everybody today seems to be in such a terrible rush, anxious for greater developments and greater riches and so on, so that children have very little time for their parents. Parents have very little time for each other, and in the home begins the disruption of peace of the world.

JANUARY 6

The most terrible poverty is loneliness and the feeling of being unloved.

JANUARY 7

If you judge people, you have no time to love them.

JANUARY 8

I know God will not give me anything I can't handle. I just wish that He didn't trust me so much.

JANUARY 9

Kind words can be short and easy to speak, but their echoes are truly endless.

JANUARY 10

Holiness does not consist in doing extraordinary things. It consists in accepting, with a smile, what Jesus sends us. It consists in accepting and following the will of God.

JANUARY 11

Prayer makes your heart bigger, until it is capable of containing the gift of God himself.

JANUARY 12

Without a spirit of sacrifice, without a life of prayer, without an intimate attitude of penance, we would not be capable of carrying out our work.

JANUARY 13

Today it is very fashionable to talk about the poor. Unfortunately, it is not fashionable to talk with them.

JANUARY 14

Peace and war begin at home. If we truly want peace in the world, let us begin by loving one another in our own families. If we want to spread joy, we need for every family to have joy.

JANUARY 15

At the moment of death we will not be judged according to the number of good deeds we have done or by the diplomas we have received in our lifetime. We will be judged according to the love we have put into our work.

JANUARY 16

To smile at someone who is sad; to visit, even for a little while, someone who is lonely; to give someone shelter from the rain with our umbrella; to read something for someone who is blind: these and others can be small things, very small things, but they are appropriate to give our love of God concrete expression.

JANUARY 17

I fear just one thing: money! Greed—the love of money—was what motivated Judas to sell Jesus.

JANUARY 18

Only God knows our true needs.

JANUARY 19

Life is an opportunity, benefit from it. Life is beauty, admire it. Life is a dream, realize it. Life is a challenge, meet it. Life is a duty, complete it. Life is a game, play it. Life is a promise, fulfill it. Life is sorrow, overcome it. Life is a song, sing it. Life is a struggle, accept it. Life is a tragedy, confront it. Life is an adventure, dare it. Life is luck, make it. Life is too precious, do not destroy it. Life is life, fight for it.

JANUARY 20

Be faithful in small things because it is in them that your strength lies.

JANUARY 21

The world is changed by your example, not your opinion.

JANUARY 22

I prefer you to make mistakes in kindness than work miracles in unkindness.

JANUARY 23

Prayer is not asking. Prayer is putting oneself in the hands of God, at His disposition, and listening to His voice in the depth of our hearts.

JANUARY 24

Being unwanted, unloved, uncared for, forgotten by everybody, I think that is a much greater hunger, a much greater poverty than the person who has nothing to eat.

JANUARY 25

Your true character is most accurately measured by how you treat those who can do nothing for you.

JANUARY 26

I want you to be concerned about your next-door neighbor. Do you know your next-door neighbor?

JANUARY 27

We think sometimes that poverty is only being hungry, naked and homeless. The poverty of being unwanted, unloved and uncared for is the greatest poverty. We must start in our own homes to remedy this kind of poverty.

JANUARY 28

When we have nothing to give, let us give Him that nothingness. Let us all remain as empty as possible, so that God can fill us.

JANUARY 29

The more you have, the more you are occupied, the less you give. But the less you have the more free you are. Poverty for us is a freedom. It is not mortification or penance. It is joyful freedom. There is no television here, no this, no that. But we are perfectly happy.

JANUARY 30

Love begins at home, and it is not how much we do . . . but how much love we put in that action.

JANUARY 31

Love cannot remain by itself—it has no meaning. Love has to be put into action, and that action is service.

February

FEBRUARY 1

God loves me. I'm not here just to fill a place, just to be a number. He has chosen me for a purpose. I know it.

FEBRUARY 2

I am not sure exactly what Heaven will be like, but I know that when we die and it comes time for God to judge us, He will not ask, "How many good things have you done in your life?" rather He will ask, "How much love did you put into what you did?"

FEBRUARY 3

Diligence, eagerness, fervor, is the test of love; and the test of fervor is the willingness to devote one's own life to working for souls. We are not attached to a single place; we are willing to go all over the world.

FEBRUARY 4

The miracle is not that we do this work, but that we are happy to do it.

FEBRUARY 5

Each person we meet is Jesus in disguise.

FEBRUARY 6

I am a little pencil in the hand of a writing God who is sending a love letter to the world.

FEBRUARY 7

I used to believe that prayer changes things, but now I know that prayer changes us, and we change things.

FEBRUARY 8

The beginning of prayer is silence. If we really want to pray we must first learn to listen, for in the silence of the heart God speaks. And to be able to see that silence, to be able to hear God we need a clean heart; for a clean heart can see God, can hear God, can listen to God; and then only from the fullness of our heart can we speak to God. But we cannot speak unless we have listened, unless we have made that connection with God in the silence of our heart.

FEBRUARY 9

I ask you one thing: do not tire of giving, but do not give your leftovers. Give until it hurts, until you feel the pain.

FEBRUARY 10

The very fact that God has placed a certain soul in our way is a sign that God wants us to do something for him or her. It is not chance; it has been planned by God. We are bound by conscience to help him or her.

FEBRUARY 11

To sometimes experience disgust is quite natural. The virtue, which at times is of heroic proportions, consists in being able to overcome disgust, for the love of Jesus. This is the secret we discover in the lives of some saints: the ability to go beyond what is merely natural.

This is what happened to Francis of Assisi. Once, when he ran into a leper who was completely disfigured, he instinctively backed up. Right away he overcame the disgust and kissed the lepers disfigured face. The leper left praising God and Francis was filled with a tremendous joy.

FEBRUARY 12

Peace begins with a smile. I will never understand all the good that a simple smile can accomplish.

FEBRUARY 13

If you can't feed a hundred people, then feed just one.

FEBRUARY 14

God doesn't require us to succeed, He only requires that you try.

FEBRUARY 15

What can you do to promote world peace? Go home and love your family.

FEBRUARY 16

Let us not be satisfied with just giving money. Money is not enough, money can be got, but they need your hearts to love them. So, spread your love everywhere you go.

FEBRUARY 17

When Jesus was dying on the Cross, He said: "I thirst." Jesus is thirsting for our love, and this is the thirst we all have, rich and poor alike. We all thirst for the love of others, that they go out of their way to avoid harming us and do good to us. This is the meaning of true love, to give until it hurts.

FEBRUARY 18

I alone cannot change the world, but I can cast a stone across the waters to create many ripples.

FEBRUARY 19

God has created us to love and to be loved, and this is the beginning of prayer—to know that He loves me, that I have been created for greater things.

FEBRUARY 20

Let me tell you something: If you feel the weight of your sins, do not be afraid! He is a loving Father; God's mercy greater than we can imagine.

FEBRUARY 21

Love can be misused for selfish motives. If I love you but at the same time I want to take from you as much as I can, even the things that are not for me to take. Then there is no true love anymore.

FEBRUARY 22

Whether one is a Hindu or a Muslim or a Christian, how you live your life is proof that you are or are not fully His. We cannot condemn or judge or pass words that will hurt people. We don't know in what way God is appearing to that soul and what God is drawing that soul to: therefore, who are we to condemn anybody?

FEBRUARY 23

If someone feels that God wants him to transform social structures, that's an issue between him and his God. We all have the duty to serve God where we feel called. I feel called to help individuals, to love each human being. I never think in terms of crowds in general but in terms of each individual person. Were I to think about crowds, I would never begin anything. It is the person that matters. I believe in person-to-person encounters.

FEBRUARY 24

Let us always meet each other with a smile, for the smile is the beginning of love.

FEBRUARY 25

Sweetest Lord, make me appreciative of the dignity of my call and its many responsibilities. Never permit me to disgrace it by giving way to coldness, unkindness, or impatience.

FEBRUARY 26

Intense love does not measure, it just gives. How intense is your love?

FEBRUARY 27

It is not the magnitude of our actions but the amount of love that is put into them that matters.

FEBRUARY 28

We have absolutely no difficulty regarding having to work in countries with many faiths. We treat all people as children of God. They are our brothers and sisters. We show great respect to them. Our work is to encourage these people, Christians as well as non-Christians, to do works of love. Every work of love done with a full heart brings people closer to God.

FEBRUARY 29

At the end of our lives we will not be judged by how many diplomas we have received, how much money we have made or how many great things we have done. We will be judged by: I was hungry and you gave me to eat. I was naked and you clothed me. I was homeless and you took me in.

March

MARCH 1

The hunger for love is much more difficult to remove than the hunger for bread.

MARCH 2

Some people come in our life as blessings. Some come in your life as lessons.

MARCH 3

Be happy in the moment, that's enough. Each moment is all we need, not more.

MARCH 4

Even the rich are hungry for love, for being cared for, for being wanted, for having someone to call their own.

MARCH 5

God is joy. Joy is prayer. Joy is a sign of generosity. When you are full of joy, you move faster and you want to go about doing good to everyone. Joy is a sign of union with God—of God's presence.

MARCH 6

Have a deep compassion for people. To be able to have a heart full of compassion we need to pray.

MARCH 7

Do you want to do something beautiful for God? There is a person who needs you. This is your chance.

MARCH 8

How do we learn to pray? When Jesus was asked by His disciples how to pray, He did not teach them methods or techniques. He said we should speak to God as a loving Father.

MARCH 9

Let us pray for peace, joy, and love. We are reminded that Jesus came to bring the good news: "My peace I leave with you, my peace I give you." He came not to give the peace of the world which is only that we do not harm each other. He came to give the peace of heart which comes from loving—from doing good to others.

MARCH 10

If you are discouraged it is a sign of pride because it shows you trust in your own power. Your self-sufficiency, your selfishness and your intellectual pride will inhibit His coming to live in your heart because God cannot fill what is already full. It is as simple as that.

MARCH 11

God is a friend of silence. The more we engage in silent prayer, the more we can give in our active life. The essential thing is not what we say to God but what God says to us and what he says through us.

MARCH 12

There are a few ways to practice humility: To speak as little as possible of one's self. To mind one's own business. Not to want to manage other people's affairs. To avoid curiosity. To accept contradictions and correction cheerfully. To pass over the mistakes of others. To accept insults and injuries. To accept being slighted, forgotten, and disliked. To be kind and gentle even under provocation.

MARCH 13

I don't know what God is doing. He knows. We do not understand, but one thing I'm sure, He doesn't make a mistake.

MARCH 14

It is not enough to say, "I love God." St. John says that you are a liar if you say you love God and you do not love your neighbor. How can you love God whom you do not see, whom you touch, with whom you live?

MARCH 15

Charity begins today. Today someone is suffering, today somebody is suffering, today somebody is in the street, today somebody is hungry. Our work is for today, yesterday has gone, tomorrow is yet to come. Do not wait for tomorrow.

MARCH 16

Make every effort to walk in the presence of God. To see God in everyone you must live your morning meditation throughout the day.

MARCH 17

My aim is to bring people closer to God.

MARCH 18

I remember my mother, my father and the rest of us praying together each evening. It is the greatest gift to a family. It maintains family unity. So go back to family prayer and teach your children to pray and pray with them.

MARCH 19

Accept whatever He gives and give whatever He takes with a big smile.

MARCH 20

Maybe in our own family we have somebody who is feeling lonely, who is feeling sick, who is feeling worried. Are we there?

MARCH 21

True love is about giving; and giving until it hurts.

MARCH 22

We do no need guns and bombs to bring peace, we need love and compassion. Let us radiate the peace of God and so light His light and extinguish all hatred and love of power in the world and in the hearts of all men.

MARCH 23

We must never think any of us is indispensable. God has His ways and means. God may allow everything to go upside down in the hands of a very talented and capable person. Unless the work is interwoven with love, it is useless.

MARCH 24

Once the longing for money comes, the longing also comes for what money can give—superfluous things. Our needs will increase, for one thing leads to another and the result will be endless dissatisfaction.

MARCH 25

Religion is not something that you or I can touch. Religion is the worship of God—therefore a matter of conscience. I alone must decide for myself and you for yourself, what we choose. For me the religion I live and use to worship God is the Catholic religion.

MARCH 26

God is always speaking to us. Listen to Him. He wants from us deep love and compassion. Feel often during the day the need for prayer. Love to pray.

MARCH 27

Unless there is forgiveness there will be no peace.

MARCH 28

The future is not in our hands. We have no power over it. We can act only today.

MARCH 29
Through prayer you will find out what God wants you to do.

MARCH 30
The most important part is that we keep the work as His work and that we do not spoil it with any claims.

MARCH 31
Today, more than ever, we need to pray for the light to know the will of God . . . for the love to accept the will of God . . . for the way to do the will of God . . .

April

APRIL 1

God has not called me to be successful, He has called me to be faithful. When we stand before God, results are not important. Faithfulness is what matters.

APRIL 2

Maybe there is a rich person who has no one to visit him; he has plenty of other things, he is nearly drowned in them, but there is not that touch and he needs your touch.

APRIL 3

The fruit of silence is prayer, the fruit of prayer is faith, the fruit of faith of love, the fruit of love is service, the fruit of service is peace.

APRIL 4

Father. God is a merciful Father. God is all powerful and He Can take care of us. God is rich in mercy and slow to anger. God is with us. God is in your heart. God is thoughtful. God is faithful. God is purity Himself. God is light. God is truth. God is joy. God is so good to us. God is a faithful lover. God is so generous and so wonderful.

APRIL 5

We have been created to love and be loved, and God has become man to make it possible for us to love as He loved us. He makes Himself the hungry one, the naked one, the homeless one, the sick one, the one in prison, the lonely one, the unwanted one . . .

APRIL 6

On the Cross Jesus said, "I thirst." He was not asking for something to drink. When they offered Him vinegar He didn't drink it . . . Very often we offer Jesus a bitter drink too. This bitterness comes from the depths of hearts and wells up in our words. When we give this bitterness to each another, we give it to Jesus.

APRIL 7

You need a deep freedom to be like Jesus. See, He could have been born in a palace, yet He chose to be poor . . . Are we so free that we can be completely naked with Jesus there on the cross?

APRIL 8

I knew that God wanted something from me. I was only twelve years old, living with my parents in Yugoslavia, when I first sense a desire.

APRIL 9

In the world there are some who struggle for justice and human rights. We have no time for this because we are in daily and continuous contact with men who are starving for a piece of bread to put in their mouth and for some affection.

APRIL 10

Let us be very sincere in our dealings with each other and have the courage to accept each other as we are. Do not be surprised at or become preoccupied with each other's failure; rather see and find the good in each other, for each one us is created in the image of God.

APRIL 11

Do we believe that God's love is infinitely more powerful, His mercy more tender than the evil of sin, than all the hatred, conflicts, and tensions that are dividing the world? Do we believe that God's love is more powerful than the most powerful bombs and guns ever made by human hands and minds?

APRIL 12

We have to love until it hurts. It is not enough to say, "I love." We must put that love into a living action. And how do we do that? By giving until it hurts.

APRIL 13

True love causes pain. Jesus, in order to give us the proof of His love, died on the cross. A mother, in order to give birth to her baby, has to suffer. If you really love one another, you will not be able to avoid making sacrifices.

APRIL 14

A beggar one day came up to me and said, "Mother Teresa, everybody gives you things for the poor. I also want to give you something, but I only have ten pence. I want to give that to you." I said to myself, "If I take it, he might have to go to bed without eating. If I don't take it, I will hurt him." So I took it. And I've never seen so much joy on anybody's face who has given food or money as I saw on that man's face that day. He was happy that he could give something. This is the joy of loving.

APRIL 15

We all have a part to play in God's glorious plans. Even if you write a letter for a blind man, or just sit and listen to someone, or you take the mail for him, and you visit somebody or bring a flower to somebody, or wash clothes for somebody or clean the house—small things, but these are great things in the eyes of God.

APRIL 16

You are a messenger of God's love, a living lamp that offers its light to all, and the salt of the earth. Take Jesus to the people and places that need Him most today.

APRIL 17

Try not to judge people. If you judge others then you are not loving them. You cannot judge and love at the same time. Instead, try to help them by seeing their needs and acting to meet them. It isn't what anyone may or may not have done, but what you have done that matters in God's eyes.

APRIL 18

The poor give us much more than we give them. They're such strong people, living day to day with no food. We don't have to give them pity or sympathy. We have so much to learn from them.

APRIL 19

My secret is very simple: I pray. Through prayer I become one in love with Christ. I realize that praying to Him is loving Him.

APRIL 20

Poverty doesn't only consist of being hungry for bread, but rather it is a tremendous hunger for human dignity. We need to love and to be somebody for somebody else. This is where we make our mistake and shove people aside. Not only have we denied the poor a piece of bread, but by thinking that they have no worth and leaving them abandoned in the streets, we have denied them the human dignity that is rightfully theirs as children of God.

APRIL 21

I cannot forget my mother. She was usually very busy all day long. But when sunset drew near, it was her custom to hurry with her tasks in order to be ready to receive my father. At the time we did not understand, and we would smile and even joke a little about it. Today I cannot help but call to mind the great delicacy of love that she had for him. No matter what happened, she was always prepared, with a smile on her lips, to welcome him.

APRIL 22

When I was crossing into Gaza, I was asked at the checkpoint whether I was carrying any weapons. I replied: Oh yes, my prayer books.

APRIL 23

I take the Lord at His word. Faith is a gift from God. Without it there would be no life. And our work, to be fruitful and beautiful, has to be built on faith. Love and faith go together. They complete each other.

APRIL 24

Nothing can make me holy except the presence of God, and to me, the presence of God is fidelity to small things. Fidelity to small things will lead you to Jesus. Infidelity to small things will lead you to sin.

APRIL 25

I must give myself completely to Him. I must not attempt to control God's actions. I must not desire a clear perception of my advance along the road, nor know precisely where I am on the way of holiness. I ask Him to make a saint of me, yet I must leave to Him the choice of the saintliness itself and still more the choice of the means that lead to it.

APRIL 26

I can't bear being photographed, but I make use of everything for the glory of God. When I allow a person to take a photograph, I tell Jesus to take one soul out of Purgatory and into Heaven.

APRIL 27

If you are really humble, if you realize how small you are and how much you need God, then you cannot fail.

APRIL 28

I am often asked, "After Mother Teresa who?" That will be no trouble. God will find someone who is more humble, more obedient, more faithful, someone with a deeper faith, and He will do still greater things through her.

APRIL 29

To know the problem of poverty intellectually is not to understand it. It is not by reading, taking a walk through the slums, that we come to understand it. We have to dive into it, live it, share it.

APRIL 30

We are commanded to love God and our neighbor equally, without difference. We don't have to look for opportunities to fill this command, they're all around us, twenty-four hours a day. You must open your eyes wide so that you can see the opportunities to give free service, wholehearted, right where you are, in your family. If you don't give such service to your family, you will not be able to give it to those outside your home.

May

MAY 1

A little child has no difficulty in loving, has no obstacles to love. And that is why Jesus said: "Unless you become like little children you cannot enter the kingdom of God."

MAY 2

When God created us, He created us out of love. There is no other explanation because God is love. And He created us to love and be loved. If we could remember that all the time, there would be no wars, no violence, no hatred in the world. So beautiful. So simple.

MAY 3

Today God continues to call—you and me—but do we listen?

MAY 4

Let us not make a mistake. The hunger of today is for Love . . . Feeding the hungry, not only for food but for the Word of God. Giving drink to the thirsty, not only for water, but for peace, truth and justice . . . nursing the sick and the dying, not only of body but also of mind and spirit.

MAY 5

Jesus has a deep and personal longing to have you for Himself.

MAY 6

Ask yourself: Have I heard Jesus say directly and personally to me, "I want your love?" If our hearts are pure, really surrendered to Him, this thing becomes part of our thirst to love Him better.

MAY 7

If we only "say" prayers then naturally you may not be praying. To pray means to be completely united to Jesus in such a way as to allow Him to pray in us, with us, for us, through us! This cleaving to each other, Jesus and I, is prayer. We are all called to pray like this.

MAY 8

Loving trust is only the fruit of total surrender. You cannot have trust unless you are one with the person. Total surrender and loving trust are twins.

MAY 9

My Jesus, do with me as you wish, as long as you wish.

MAY 10

See the humility of God. He made Himself the hungry one to satisfy our hunger . . . See the unity between prayer and wholehearted free service. We meet Jesus in the Bread of Life in the Eucharist and the humanity of Christ in the distressing disguise of the poor. We are called to unite both of these . . . Prayer by itself—No! Work by itself—No! These two belong together.

MAY 11

I remember when I was leaving home fifty years ago—my mother was dead set against me leaving home and becoming a sister. In the end when she realized that this was what God wanted from me, she said something very strange: "Put your hand in His hand and walk all alone with Him." I didn't understand it at the time, but this is life. We may be surrounded by many people, yet our vocation is really lived out alone with Jesus.

MAY 12

For twenty years, I was at work in education at St. Mary's High School. I love teaching, and in Loreto I was the happiest nun in the world.

MAY 13

Twenty years after I came to India, I actually decided upon this close contact with the poor. I felt that God wanted from me something more.

MAY 14

Don't allow anything to interfere with your love for Jesus. You belong to Him. Nothing can separate you from Him. That one sentence is important to remember. He will be your joy, your strength. If you hold onto that sentence, temptations and difficulties will come, but nothing will break you. Remember, you have been created for great things.

MAY 15

Don't search for Jesus in far lands—He is not there. He is close to you; He is with you. Just keep the lamp burning and you will; always see Him. Keep on filling the lamp with all these little drops of love, and you will see how sweet is the Lord you love.

MAY 16

We are able to go through the most terrible places fearlessly, because Jesus is in us. Jesus is our joy, our strength, our joy, and our compassion.

MAY 17

Jesus loved us to the end, to the very limit, dying on the cross. We must have this same love which comes from within, from our union with Jesus. This love should be as normal to us as living and breathing.

MAY 18

Love is not about patronizing and charity isn't about pity, it is about pouring ourselves out for others. Charity and love are the same—with charity you give love, so don't just give money but reach out your hand also.

MAY 19

We should ask ourselves, Have I really experienced the joy of loving? True love is love that causes pain, that hurts, and yet brings joy. This is why we pray asking for the courage to love, and love more deeply than ever before.

MAY 20

To do God's work you need a few things. We need health of mind and body. We need the ability to learn. We need plenty of common sense and a cheerful disposition. I think common sense and cheerfulness are very necessary if we are to bring God's love to as many people as possible.

MAY 21

We are called to cultivate that sacred silence which makes people remember the words of Jesus: See how they love one another. How often we find ourselves speaking about the faults of another. How often our conversation is about someone who is not present. Yet see the compassion of Christ toward Judas, the man who received so much love yet betrayed his own master. But the master kept the sacred silence and did not betray Judas. Jesus could have easily spoken in public—as we often do —telling the hidden intentions and deeds of Judas to others. But He didn't. Instead, He showed mercy and charity. Rather than condemning Judas, He called him His friend.

MAY 22

In many places, children are neglected, but animals are cared for and pampered. Animals are given special food and other special things. I love dogs myself, very much, but still I cannot bear seeing a dog given the place of a child.

MAY 23

To parents: It is very important that children learn from their fathers and mothers how to love one another. Not in school, not from the teacher, but from you. It is very important that you share with your children the joy of loving others. There will be misunderstandings. Every family has its cross, its suffering, but always be the first to forgive with a smile. Be cheerful, be happy.

MAY 24

Everything we do each day is a means to put our love for Christ into living loving action. It is so beautiful that we complete each other. What we are doing in the slums, maybe you cannot do. What you are doing where you are called—in your family, in your life at college, in your work—we cannot do. But you and we together are doing something beautiful for God.

MAY 25

Choose the way of peace. Let us not use bombs and guns to overcome the world. Let us use love and compassion. Peace begins with a smile. Smile five times a day at someone you don't really want to smile at all. Do it for peace. Let us radiate the peace of God. In this way let us set the world alight with His light and extinguish all hatred and love of power. Peace in the world, yes, but first peace in our hearts. Do you have peace in your heart today? If not, why not?

MAY 26

Be faithful to the time spent in prayer and make sure that at least half of your prayer is spent in silence. This will bring you closer to Jesus. If you deepen your prayer life you will grow in holiness and obtain many graces for the souls entrusted to your care. Deepen your love for one another by praying for each other and by sharing thoughts and graces you have received in prayer and reading.

MAY 27

You are called to be holy where you are, wherever God has put you, right now.

MAY 28

Resist anything that leads to moodiness. Our prayer each day should be, "Let the joy of the Lord be my strength." Cheerfulness and joy were Mary's strength. This made her a willing handmaid of God. Only joy could have given her the strength to go in haste over the hills of Judea to her cousin Elizabeth, there to do the work of a handmaid. If we are to be true handmaids of the Lord, then we too, each day, must go cheerfully in haste over the hills of difficulty.

MAY 29

We are here to be witnesses of love and to celebrate life, because life has been created in the image of God. Life is to love and to be loved. That's why we all have to take a strong stand so that no child —boy or girl—will be rejected or unloved. Every child is a sign of God's love.

MAY 30

Our life of poverty is as necessary as the work itself. Only in heaven will we see how much we owe to the poor for helping us to love God better because of them.

MAY 31

Every day is a preparation for death. By realizing this, it helps somehow, because we each have to die a little each day. Death is nothing except going back to Him, where He is and where we belong.

June

JUNE 1

One man told me: "I am an atheist," but he spoke so beautifully about love. Mother told me: "You cannot be an atheist if you speak so beautifully about love." Where there is love, there is God. God is love.

JUNE 2

If you are hungry to hear the voice of God, you will hear. To hear, you have to cut out all other things.

JUNE 3

Let us offer everything to Jesus—every sorrow, humiliation, discomfort. In this way, you too, can take your stand at the foot of the Cross with Mary, our Mother.

JUNE 4

Mary allowed God to take possession of her life by her purity, her humility, and her faithful love. She did it so beautifully. Let us seek to grow, under the guidance of our Heavenly Mother, in these three important interior attitudes of the soul that delight the heart of God and enable Him to unite Himself to us.

JUNE 5

The thirst of Jesus on the Cross is not imagination. "I thirst," He said. Hear Him saying it to you . . . and respond.

JUNE 6

I was travelling by train to Darjeeling when I heard the voice of God. I was sure it was God's voice. I was certain He was calling me to something more. The message was clear.

JUNE 7

If the poor die of hunger, it is not because God does not care for them. Rather, it is because neither you nor I are generous enough. It is because we are not instruments of love in the hands of God. We do not recognize Christ when once again He appears to us in the hungry man, in the lonely woman, in the child who is looking for a place to get warm.

JUNE 8

At times, I feel rather sad, because we do so little. Most people praise us for our actions, but what we do is not more than a drop of water in the ocean. It hardly affects the immensity of human suffering.

JUNE 9

Some people would advise me to change certain things. For instance, they tell me that the sisters should have fans in the common room or in the chapel. I do not want them to have fans. The poor whom they are to serve have no fans. The same is true for the routine of the house. I always ask the people, "Please do not interfere!"

JUNE 10

Try to put in the hearts of your children a love for home. Make them long to be with their families. So much sin could be avoided if only people really loved as family.

JUNE 11

People often ask me, "You work to bring about peace, why don't you work to lessen war?" If we work for peace there will be fewer wars. But I won't mix our work with politics. War is the fruit of politics, and so I don't involve myself, that's all. If I get stuck in politics, I will stop loving, because I will have to stand by one, and not by all.

JUNE 12

To students: I pray that all those young people who have graduated, do not carry just a piece of paper with them but that they carry with them love, peace, and joy. That they become the sunshine of God's love to our people, the hope of eternal happiness, and the burning flame of love wherever they go. That they become carriers of God's love. That they be able to give what they have received. For they have received not to keep but to share.

JUNE 13

Every human being comes from the hand of God, and we all know something of God's love for us through each person we encounter. Whatever our religion, we know that if we really want to love, we must first, before anything else, learn to forgive.

JUNE 14

Let us not be satisfied with giving money. Money is not everything. The poor need more than our money. The poor need the work of our hands and the love of our hearts. Love—the abundant love of God alive in you and me—is the beautiful expression of our Christian religion.

JUNE 15

Some in our country call God Ishwar. Others call him Allah. And others just call Him God. Every one of us has to recognize that He created us for greater things, such as to love and be loved. Who are we to keep our people from looking for God who has created them, who loves them, and to whom we all must return one day?

JUNE 16

Riches can suffocate if they are not used in the right way, whether they are spiritual riches or material.

JUNE 17

Holiness is not something extraordinary, not something for only a few. Holiness is for every one of us. It is a simple duty: the acceptance of God with a smile, at all times, anywhere and everywhere.

JUNE 18

Offer God all your words and all your actions. Everything for God. Everything with God.

JUNE 19

Never waste a chance to become more like Jesus.

JUNE 20

Our lives have to continuously feed on the Eucharist. If we were not able to see Christ under the appearance of bread, neither would it be possible for us to discover Him under the humble appearances of the bruised bodies of the poor.

JUNE 21

How can you truly know the poor unless you live like them? If they complain about the food, we can say that we eat the same. The more we have the less we can give. Poverty is a wonderful gift because it gives us freedom—it means we have fewer obstacles to God.

JUNE 22

The woman is the heart of the home. Let us pray that we realize the reason for our existence: to love and be loved and through this love become instruments of peace in the world.

JUNE 23

A joyful heart is the normal result of heart burning with love. Joy is not simply a matter of temperament. It is always hard to remain joyful—all the more reason why we should try to acquire it and encourage it grow in our hearts.

JUNE 24

Mary showed complete trust in God by agreeing to be used as an instrument in His plan. She trusted Him in spite of her nothingness, because she knew He could do great things in her and through her. Once she said "yes" to God, Mary never doubted. She was just a young woman, but she belonged to God and nothing nor anyone could separate her from Him.

JUNE 25

I once picked up a small girl who was wandering the streets, lost. Hunger was written all over her face. Who knows how long it had been since she had eaten anything! I offered her a piece of bread. The little one started eating, crumb by crumb. I told her, "Eat, eat the bread!" She looked at me and said, " I am just afraid that when I run out of bread, I'll still be hungry."

JUNE 26

I always begin my prayer in silence, for it is in the silence of the heart that God speaks. God and silence are great friends. We need to listen to God, because it's not what we say, but what He says to us and through us that matters.

JUNE 27

There is so much suffering in the world—physical, material, mental. The suffering of some can be blamed on the greed of others. The material and physical suffering is suffering from hunger, from homelessness, from all kinds of diseases. Will we allow greed to rule our hearts or will we accept God's invitation to joyful generosity?

JUNE 28

When someone is doing something to hurt you, don't turn inward, turn toward that person. He is hurting himself. Learn to forgive, knowing that we all need forgiveness. If you want to be true to God, learn from Jesus to be meek, humble, and pure. Learn to forgive.

JUNE 29

Should I devote myself to struggle for the justice of tomorrow or even for the justice of today, the most needy people would die right in front of me because they lack a glass of milk . . . I do not condemn those who struggle for justice. I believe there are different options for the people of God. To me the most important thing is to serve the neediest people.

JUNE 30

To leave Loreto was my greatest sacrifice, the most difficult thing I have ever done. It was much more difficult than to leave my family and country. In Loreto I have received my spiritual training.

July

JULY 1

Everybody today seems to be in a hurry. No one has any time to give to others: children to their parents; parents to their children; spouses to each other.

JULY 2

God created the whole world, but He is our Father. The Father loves me, and you. The tenderness of God's love—no one can love as God. He made us. He is Our Father.

JULY 3

What is prayer? Prayer is oneness with God.

JULY 4

If you listen with your heart, you will hear and you will understand . . . Until you know deep inside that Jesus thirsts for you, you cannot begin to know who He wants to be for you. Or who He wants you to be for Him.

JULY 5

We are contemplatives in the heart of the world . . . Whatever we are, whatever we do, it is not what we do, but how much love we put into it. How much love!

JULY 6

Don't be afraid to be small. Numbers are not what make a difference, but—are we really His?

JULY 7

One of the most beautiful gifts that God has given me is to serve and put my love for Jesus in living action as I serve the poorest of the poor... in giving tender love and care to the poor, to the dying, to the crippled, to the unwanted, to the unloved, to the lepers, and so bring new life and new joy into their lives.

JULY 8

On my first trip along the streets of Calcutta, a priest came up to me. He asked me to give a contribution to a collection for the Catholic press. I had left with five rupees, and I had already given four of them to the poor. I hesitated, then gave the priest the one that remained. That afternoon, the same priest came to see me and brought an envelope. He told me that a man had given him the envelope because he had heard about my projects and wanted to help me. There were fifty rupees in that envelope. I had the felling, at that moment, that God had begun to bless the work and would never abandon me.

JULY 9

One by one, my former students began to arrive. They wanted to give everything to God. With what joy they put away their colorful saris in order to put on our poor cotton one.

JULY 10

Once we take our eyes away from ourselves, from our interests, from our own rights, privileges, ambitions—then they will become clear to see Jesus around us.

JULY 11

A high-ranking government official once said to me, "You are doing social work and we also do the same. But we are doing it for something and you are doing it for somebody." To do our work we have to be in love with God.

JULY 12

It is much easier to conquer a country than to conquer ourselves.

JULY 13

Every act of love is a work of peace, no matter how small.

JULY 14

I don't claim anything of the work. It's His work. I'm like a little pencil in His hand. That's all. He does the thinking. He does the writing. The pencil has nothing to do with it. The pencil has only to be allowed to be used.

JULY 15

Rigorous poverty is our safeguard. We do not want, as has been the case with other religious orders throughout history, to begin serving the poor and then gradually move toward serving the rich. In order for us to understand and to be able to help those who lack everything, we have to live as they live. The difference lies only in the fact that those we aid are poor by force, whereas we are poor by choice.

JULY 16

We are entirely at the disposal of the Church. We profess a deep personal love for the Holy Father. We surrender ourselves completely to be united with Him as carriers of God's love. Pray for us that we don't spoil the work God has called us to do.

JULY 17

Do not wait for leaders; do it alone, person to person. Today.

JULY 18

Abandonment is an awful poverty. There are poor people everywhere, but the deepest poverty is not being loved.

JULY 19

I have seen every disease. I have seen people suffer in unimaginable ways. But I tell you, one of the greatest diseases is to be nobody to anybody.

JULY 20

We know only too well that what we are doing is nothing more than a drop in the ocean in the whole scheme of things, but not for the people we serve. So, our work may be just a drop in the ocean, but if that drop were not there, the ocean would be missing something.

JULY 21

I have met many famous people, successful people, wealthy people, and powerful people. None of us—not you, or me, or them—ever do great things. But we can all do small things with great love, and together we can do something wonderful.

JULY 22

Be kind and merciful. Let no one ever come to you without coming away better and happier. Be a living expression of God's kindness.

JULY 23

I have never been in a war, but I have seen famine, death, and destruction. I was asking myself the other day: What do people feel when they provoke war? I don't understand it. We are all children of God. In every war, on both sides, everyone involved, everyone affected is a child of God.

JULY 24

All of us are called to work in a special way for the sake of peace. In order to bring about that peace, we need to learn from Jesus to be meek and humble of heart. Only humility will lead us to unity, and unity to peace.

JULY 25

I believe that many people today think the poor are not humans like them. They look down on them. But if they had a deep respect for the poor, I am sure it would be easy for them to come closer to them, and to see that they have as much right to the things of life and to love as anybody has.

JULY 26

I feel that we too often focus on the negative aspects of life, on what is bad. If we were more willing to see the good and the beautiful things that surround us we would be able to transform society. It begins in the family. From there, we can help transform our next-door neighbors with loving service, then others who live in our neighborhood and city. We can bring peace and love to the world. The whole world is hungry for these things, and we can each play a small role in feeding this great hunger.

JULY 27

Live life beautifully. You have Jesus with you, and He loves you. If we could only remember that God loves us, and we have an opportunity to love others as He loves us. Not in big things, but in small things with great love, then your country will become a haven of peace and a burning light of love in the world.

JULY 28

We must know that we have been created for greater things, not just to be a number in the world, not just to go for degrees and diplomas. Not just to work and accomplish. We have been created to love and to be loved. This is easy to forget amidst the busyness of life. You have been created to love and to be loved. Make love a priority.

JULY 29

Prayer is necessary as air to breathe, as necessary as the blood in our bodies, as necessary as anything. We think so many things are necessary, but we are wrong. We have been deceived and we deceive ourselves. So few things are necessary, and prayer is one of them.

JULY 30

Serve God joyfully. Let there be no sadness in your life. The only true sorrow is sin.

JULY 31

Bring God to everyone you meet each day. Humility always radiates the glory and greatness of God. How wonderful are the ways of God who chose humility, smallness, helplessness, and poverty to prove His love to the world. Do not be afraid to be humble, small, and helpless in order to prove your love for God and others.

August

AUGUST 1

One day right in the beginning, we had no rice for dinner and then a lady came and brought rice. She said she was coming back from the office "and something in me told me to go to Mother Teresa and bring her rice." How beautiful it is when we listen to the Holy Spirit.

AUGUST 2

If our life is without prayer, it is like a house without a foundation.

AUGUST 3

The sound of your footsteps in search of souls to love should be like sweet music for Jesus. Keep the thirst for souls ever burning in your hearts.

AUGUST 4

Until you hear Jesus in the silence of your heart, you will not be able to hear Him saying, "I thirst" in the hearts of the poor . . .

AUGUST 5

When a young woman of high caste comes and puts herself at the service of the poor, she is the protagonist of a revolution. It is the greatest, the most difficult revolution—the revolution of love.

AUGUST 6

Love is a fruit in season at all times, and within reach of every hand. Anyone may gather it and no limit is set.

AUGUST 7

I see God in every human being. When I wash the leper's wounds I feel I am nursing the Lord Himself. Is that not a beautiful experience?

AUGUST 8

It is easy to smile at people outside your own home. It is so easy to take care of the people that you don't know well. It is difficult to be thoughtful and kind and to smile and be loving to those you live with day after day. This is especially true when we are tired and in a bad temper or bad mood. We all have these moments and that is the time that Christ comes to us in a distressing disguise.

AUGUST 9

If peace and love are not allowed to take their rightful place at the table of negotiation, then hatred and anger will produce conflict that will continue for many years to come. It will solve nothing, and thousands of innocent lives will be lost. I ask you all to pray for peace. It is such an urgent priority.

AUGUST 10

If you are humble, nothing will touch you. Neither praise nor disgrace, because you know what you are. If you are blamed, you won't be discouraged; if anyone calls you a saint, you won't put yourself on a pedestal.

AUGUST 11

If you are kind, people may accuse you of ulterior motives. Be kind anyway.

AUGUST 12

Sacrifice, surrender, and suffering are not popular topics today. Our culture makes us believe that we can have it all, that we should demand our rights, that with the right technology all pain and problems can be overcome. That is not my attitude toward sacrifice.

AUGUST 13

God told us, "Love your neighbor as yourself." So first I am to love myself rightly, and then to love my neighbor like that. But how can I love myself unless I accept myself as God has made me? Those who deny that beautiful differences between men and women are not accepting themselves as God has made them, and so cannot accept and love their neighbor. They will only bring division, unhappiness, and destruction of peace to the world.

AUGUST 14

I am convinced that today's youth are more generous than those of times past. Our youth are better prepared and more willing to sacrifice to serve others.

AUGUST 15

Don't come to prayer looking for extraordinary experiences. Come to visit your great friend Jesus, always present and waiting for you in the tabernacle. This is the friendship that strengthens us to fulfill our day-to-day ordinary duties with extraordinary love and devotion.

AUGUST 16

If you are successful you will win some false friends and true enemies: Succeed anyway.

AUGUST 17

Stay where you are. Find your own Calcutta. Find the sick, the suffering, and the lonely right where you are—in your own homes and in your own families, in your workplaces and in your schools.

AUGUST 18

It is much easier to conquer a country than to conquer ourselves. Every act of disobedience weakens my spiritual life. It is like a wound letting out every drop of one's blood. Nothing can cause havoc in our spiritual life as quickly as disobedience.

AUGUST 19

Let us insist more and more on raising funds of love, of kindness, of understanding, of peace. Money will come. If we seek first the Kingdom of God—the rest will be given.

AUGUST 20

We too are called to withdraw at certain intervals into deeper silence and aloneness with God, together as a community as well as personally. To be alone with Him—not with our books, thoughts, and memories but completely stripped of everything—to dwell lovingly in His presence. Silent, empty, expectant, and motionless. We cannot find God in noise or agitation.

AUGUST 21

"Mother, how can you remain so joyful surrounded by all this suffering and aware that so many are indifferent?" The question always makes me smile. Jesus is the source of my joy, not anything in this world. I go to prayer, every day, so He can fill me with His joy. When I am weary and discouraged, I go and sit with Jesus. He invited us to do that. "Come to me, all you who are weary and burdened, and I will give you rest. Take my yoke upon you and learn from me, for I am gentle and humble of heart, and you will find rest for your souls. For my yoke is easy and my burden is light."

AUGUST 22

Mary did not feel ashamed. She proclaimed Jesus her son. At Calvary we see her standing upright—the mother of God, standing next to the cross. What a deep faith she must have had because of her love for her son! To see Him dishonored, unloved, and object of hatred. Yet, she stayed upright.

AUGUST 23

Here is another paradox: When you don't have anything, then you have everything. Having nothing liberates you in unimaginable ways. Be careful what you become attached to. In the end we have to give it all up anyway. But it is not true that we leave this world with nothing just as we came into the world with nothing. We can't take things or money with us, but we take all the love we have allowed God to fill us with.

AUGUST 24

We fear the future because we are wasting the today.

AUGUST 25

so helpless and weak. I think that is why God uses me, because I cannot depend on my own strength. I rely on Him twenty-four hours a day. If the day had even more hours, then I would need His help and grace during those hours too. I cling to Him in prayer, and I encourage you to do the same.

AUGUST 26

Each one of us is merely a small instrument. All of us, after accomplishing our mission, will disappear. The only question is: Will you collaborate with God so He can use you to do His work here on earth?

AUGUST 27

What you spend years building, someone could destroy overnight: Build anyway.

AUGUST 28

If you hear of someone who doesn't want to have her child, who wants to have an abortion, try to convince her to bring the child to me. I will love that child, who is a sign of God's love... I don't think any human heart should dare to take life, or any human hand be raised to destroy life. Life is the life of God in us. Life is the greatest gift that God has bestowed on human beings, and man has been created in the image of God. Life belongs to God, and we have no right to destroy it.

AUGUST 29

The greatest disease in the West today is not tuberculosis or leprosy; it is being unwanted, unloved, and uncared for. We can cure physical diseases with medicine, but the only cure for loneliness, despair, and hopelessness is love. There are so many people in the world who are dying for a piece of bread, but there are many more people dying for a little love. The poverty in the West is a different kind of poverty—it is not only a poverty of loneliness but also a profound spirituality poverty. There's a hunger for love, as there is a hunger for God.

AUGUST 30

Lord, Grant that I may always bear in mind the very great dignity of the life you have called me to and all its responsibilities. Never let me dishonor it by being cold, or unkind, or impatient.

AUGUST 31

Jesus loves you. Even more—He longs for you. He misses you when you don't come close. He thirsts for you, even when you don't feel worthy.

September

SEPTEMBER 1

Be a soul of prayer. If we don't learn to pray, all of our life will be handicapped.

SEPTEMBER 2

If you want to become holy, become poor. Jesus became poor to save us, and if we really want to become poor, like Jesus, then we have to be really poor, spiritually poor.

SEPTEMBER 3

When we speak of the poorest of the poor, who comes to mind? Who are the poorest of the poor? Nobody but you and me! We are the poorest of the poor.

SEPTEMBER 4

That terrible longing keeps growing and I feel as if something will break in me one day—and then that darkness comes, that loneliness, that feeling of terrible aloneness. Heaven seems closed from every side —and yet I long for God. I long to love Him with every drop of life in me—and I want to love Him with a deep personal love.

SEPTEMBER 5

The reason I was given the Nobel Prize was because of the poor. The prize, however, went beyond appearances. In fact, it awakened consciences in favor of the poor all over the world. It became a sort of reminder that the poor are our brothers and sisters, and that we have the duty to treat them with love.

SEPTEMBER 6

We care for thousands of lepers. They are among the most unwanted, unloved, and neglected people. The other day one of our sisters was washing a leper covered with sores. A Muslim holy man was present, standing close to her. He said, "All these years I have believed that Jesus Christ is a prophet. Today I believe that Jesus Christ is God since He has been able to give such joy to this sister, so that she can do her work with so much love."

SEPTEMBER 7

Sometimes people are hungry for more than bread. It is possible that our children, our husband, our wife, do not hunger for bread, do not need clothes, do not lack a house. But are we equally sure that they do not feel alone, abandoned, neglected, or in need of some affection?

SEPTEMBER 8

Give Jesus a big smile each time your nothingness frightens you. Just keep the joy of Jesus as your strength—be happy and at peace, accept whatever He gives or takes with a big smile.

SEPTEMBER 9

At the very beginning, after leaving my convent at Loreto, when I arrived in Calcutta I was alone. I had only a box and five rupees. A man from Air India wanted to give me a nice suitcase to carry the few things I had with me. I said to him, "There is no shame in carrying a cardboard box." But there is no shame in asking when we need guidance or help.

SEPTEMBER 10

You are the future of family life. You are the future of the joy of loving. You are the future of making your life something beautiful for God . . . That you love a girl or that you love a boy is beautiful, but don't spoil it, don't destroy it. Ask God to guide you in your love.

SEPTEMBER 11

I heard the Pope John Paul II speak about peace, and one thing he said was this: "No to violence and yes to peace." What is violence? In the first place, we think of weapons, knives, killings. We never think of connecting violence with our tongues. But the first weapon, the cruelest weapon, is the tongue. Examine what part your tongue has played in creating peace or violence. We can really wound a person, we can kill a person, with our tongue.

SEPTEMBER 12

Prayer is not about asking for things. Prayer is about putting yourself in the hands of God. Make yourself available to Him and learn to listen to His voice in the depths of your heart.

SEPTEMBER 13

There is a light in this world, a healing spirit more powerful than any darkness we may encounter. We sometimes lose sight of this force when there is suffering. The pain we witness can be overwhelming. Then suddenly, the Spirit will emerge through the lives of ordinary people who hear a call and answer with extraordinary love.

SEPTEMBER 14

If you find serenity and happiness, they may be jealous of you: Be happy anyway.

SEPTEMBER 15

You can pray while you work. Work doesn't stop prayer and prayer doesn't stop work. It requires only that small raising of the mind to Him: I love you God, I trust you, I believe in you, I need you now. Small things like that. These are wonderful ways to pray and wonderful prayers.

SEPTEMBER 16

We are all called to live contemplative lives. Contemplation is not to be shut up in a dark place, but to allow Jesus to live His passion, love, and humility in us, praying with us, being with us, sanctifying us and others through us.

SEPTEMBER 17

We learn humility through accepting humiliations cheerfully. Do not let a chance pass you by. It is so easy to be proud, harsh, moody, and selfish, but we have been created for greater things. Why stoop down to things that will spoil the beauty of our hearts?

SEPTEMBER 18

Confess your sin and be finished with it. God's mercy is greater than your sin. Don't be afraid, scrupulous, or anxious. You are a sinner full of sin when you go to Confession, and when you come out you are a sinner without sin. But always, before everything else and after everything else, you are a child of God.

SEPTEMBER 19

What are you hiding? What do you do in secret? Doing things in secret, hiding, these things are the beginning of lying.

SEPTEMBER 20

Forgiveness is at the heart of healthy relationships. Excuse rather than accuse. Forgive and ask to be forgiven. Forgiveness is a beautiful gift to give to those who hurt us.

SEPTEMBER 21

In the West you have another kind of poverty, spiritual poverty. This is far worse. People do not believe in God, do not pray. People do not care for each other. You have the poverty of people who are dissatisfied with what they have, who do not know how to suffer, who give in to despair. This poverty of heart is often more difficult to relieve and to defeat.

SEPTEMBER 22

Joy is very infectious. We will never know just how much good a simple smile can do. Be faithful in little things. Smile at the people who cross your path. You have a beautiful smile. Don't waste it. Live beautifully. Smile at life. Smile everywhere you go. Smile at everyone you meet.

SEPTEMBER 23

Money? I never give it a thought. It always comes. We work for Jesus. It is His work and He will provide. He has always taken care of us. If He wants something to be done, He will give us the means. If He does not provide us with the means, then it shows that He doesn't want that particular work. So, I forget about it.

SEPTEMBER 24

Many people who have many possessions, who have many goods and riches, are obsessed with them. They think that the only thing that counts is possessing wealth. That is why it is so difficult for them to walk each moment of each day with God. Too many of their moments are spent preoccupied with money and things.

SEPTEMBER 25

No matter how tired you are, no matter how physically exhausting your life may be, make it a priority to care for someone in need. What greater joy can there be?

SEPTEMBER 26

I believe God loves the world through us—through you and me.

SEPTEMBER 27

God created us to love and be loved, and so we hunger for chances to love and be loved. The hunger for love is much more difficult to remove than the hunger for bread.

SEPTEMBER 28

Everything starts with prayer. Everything good thing we do flows from prayer. Ask God to fill you with His love so you can take His love out into the world and share it with others. We talk about prayer at church, but are we praying? It is easy to talk about the poor, but talking about the poor is not the same as talking to the poor. It is easy to talk about prayer, but talking about prayer is not the same as sitting down in a quiet place and talking to God.

SEPTEMBER 29

Living a Christian life provides for the growth of faith. There have been many saints who have gone before to guide us, but I like the ones who are simple, like St. Therese of Lisieux. I chose her as my namesake because she did ordinary things with extraordinary love.

SEPTEMBER 30

Death is the most decisive moment in human life. It is like our coronation: to die in peace with God.

October

OCTOBER 1

If we really want to love, we must learn to forgive.

OCTOBER 2

When we touch the sick and needy, we touch the suffering body of Christ.

OCTOBER 3

Joy is prayer; joy is strength: joy is love; joy is a net of love by which you can catch souls.

OCTOBER 4

Meditation is talking to Jesus. It is a deep intimate conversation with Jesus.

OCTOBER 5

From the cross Jesus cries out, "I thirst." His thirst was for souls even as He hung there dying, alone, despised. Who will bring those souls to Him? Can you and I continue to stand by as mere spectators? Can we pass by and do nothing?

OCTOBER 6

Look at Mary Magdalene; she was so in love in Jesus. She went early in the morning to see Him . . . Are we like that at holy Mass? During Prayer? Do we have that eagerness and longing to be with Him?

OCTOBER 7

When you look at the inner workings of electrical things, you often see small and big wires, new and old, cheap and expensive, all lined up. Until the current passes through them there will be no light. That wire is you and me. The current is God. We have the power to let the current pass through us, use us, produce the light of the world. Or we can refuse to be used and allow darkness to spread.

OCTOBER 8

You and I are called to do very humble work. There are many people who can do big things, but there are very few people who will do the small things.

OCTOBER 9

Charity for the poor is like a living flame; the drier the fuel, the brighter it burns. In your service to the poor do not give only your hands but also your hearts. Charity to be fruitful must cost us. Give, give, give. Give until it hurts. To love, it is necessary to give: to give it is necessary to be free from selfishness.

OCTOBER 10

Bring love into your homes. If you truly love God, start loving your son or your daughter and your spouse. And the elderly, where are they? In nursing homes! Why are they not with you? And where is the retarded child? In an institution! Why is he not with you? That child is a gift from God.

OCTOBER 11

A gentleman of the Protestant faith told me: "I love you; I love your work; and I love everything I see here. But there is one thing I don't understand: Our Lady. You are full of Mary." This is not difficult to understand I explained to him: "No Mary, no Jesus. No mother, no son. I know you love Jesus. Loving and respecting the women who brought Him into this world is a natural extension of your love for Jesus. Loving Mary is not exclusively Catholic." A few months later he sent me a card with these words printed in big letters: "I believe, No Mary, no Jesus! This has changed my life."

OCTOBER 12

The constitutions of our religious order state: "We and our poor will rely entirely on divine providence. We are not ashamed to beg from door to door as members of Christ, who Himself lived on alms during His public life and whom we serve in the sick and poor."

OCTOBER 13

Faith in action is service. We try to be holy because we believe. In most modern rooms you see an electrical light that can be turned on by a switch. But if there is no connection with the main powerhouse, then there can be no light. Faith and prayer are our connection with God, and power of that connection is service.

OCTOBER 14

Every moment of prayer, especially before our Lord in the tabernacle, is a sure, positive gain. The time we spend each day sitting with God is the most precious part of the whole day.

OCTOBER 15

Suffering is an inevitable part of life. When suffering comes to us, let us accept it with a smile. This is one of the greatest gifts God has given us: the courage to accept with a smile whatever He gives, whatever He allows, whatever He takes.

OCTOBER 16

If you were to die today, what would others say about you? What was in you that was beautiful, that was Christlike, that helped others to pray better? Face yourself, with Jesus at your side, and do not be satisfied with just any answer. Go deep into the question. Examine your life.

OCTOBER 17

When we realize that we are all sinners needing forgiveness, it will be easier for us to forgive others. We have to be forgiven in order to be able to forgive. If I do not understand this, it will be very hard for me to say, "I forgive you" to anyone.

OCTOBER 18

Material riches and spiritual riches can both choke you if you do not use them fairly. For not even God can put anything in a heart that is already full. One day there springs up the desire for money and for all that money can provide: superfluous luxury. Eating fine meals, the finest clothes, luxury homes, expensive vacations. These things are trifles. One desire leads to another, and then we begin to think that we need these things. The result is uncontrollable dissatisfaction. Let us live simply and remain as empty as possible so that God can fill us up.

OCTOBER 19

Life is an adventure, dare it.

OCTOBER 20

If we were truly humble, nothing would change us—neither praise or discouragement. If someone were to criticize us, we would not feel discouraged. If someone would praise us, we also would not feel proud.

OCTOBER 21

Bring love into your homes. If you truly love God, start loving your son or your daughter and your spouse. And the elderly, where are they? In nursing homes! Why are they not with you? And where is the retarded child? In an institution! Why is he not with you? That child is a gift from God.

OCTOBER 22

God allows failure, but He does not want us to become discouraged. God doesn't require us to succeed, He only requires that you try.

OCTOBER 23

Do not think that love, in order to be genuine, has to be extraordinary. What we need is to love without getting tired.

OCTOBER 24

People remind me of what a magazine once said about me. It described me as a "living saint." If someone sees God in me, I am happy. I see God in everyone, especially in those who suffer. And I remind myself of what Francis of Assisi said, "I am who I am in the eyes of God, and nothing more."

OCTOBER 25

I think that a person who is attached to riches, who lives with the worry of riches, is actually very poor. If this person puts his money at the service of others, then he is rich, very rich.

OCTOBER 26

The most appealing invitation to walk with God is the witness of our own lives, the spirit with which we respond to our divine calling, the completeness of our dedication, the generosity and cheerfulness of our service to God, and the love we have for one another.

OCTOBER 27

People die suddenly all the time, so it could happen to us at any moment. Yesterday is gone and tomorrow has not yet come; we must live each day as if it were our last, so that when God calls us we are ready to go home to God with a clean heart.

OCTOBER 28

Joy is a sign of a generous personality. Sometimes it is also a mantle that clothes a life of great sacrifice and self-giving. A person who has the gift of joy often reaches high summits.

OCTOBER 29

One cannot expect to become a saint without paying the price, and the price is much renunciation, much temptation, much struggle and persecution, and all sorts of sacrifices. One cannot love God except at the cost of oneself.

OCTOBER 30

When I pick up a hungry person from the street, I give him a plate of rice, a piece of bread. But a person who is shut out, who feels unwanted unloved, terrified, the person who has been thrown out of society—that spiritual poverty is much harder to overcome.

OCTOBER 31

All my years of service to the poor have helped me to understand that they are precisely the ones who better understand human dignity. If they have a problem, it is not lack of money, but the fact that their right to be treated humanely and with tenderness is not recognized.

November

NOVEMBER 1

Before you speak, it is necessary for you listen, for God speaks in the silence of the heart.

NOVEMBER 2

Silence of the heart. This is what will allow you to hear God everywhere: in the closing of a door, in the person who needs you, in the birds that sing, in the flowers.

NOVEMBER 3

If I had to start all over again, I would do the same thing. I have experienced many human weaknesses, many human frailties, and I still experience them.

NOVEMBER 4

Whoever the poorest of the poor are, they are Christ for us. Jesus under the guise of human suffering.

NOVEMBER 5

Bring prayer back into your family life and you will experience unity—and a joyful love that will bind you together. Maybe there is suffering in your family, but praying together, sharing together, loving together will help you.

NOVEMBER 6

No one can take my faith from me. If in order to spread the love of Jesus among the poor and neglected, there were no alternative but to remain in a country that despises Christianity, I would remain. But I would not renounce my faith. I am prepared to give up my life, but never my faith.

NOVEMBER 7

Young people are full of love and strength, do not waste your energy on useless things. Look around and you will see your brother and your sister, not only here in the United States, not only in your city or your area, but around the world. Everywhere there are human beings who are hungry, they look to you. There are so many who have nothing to wear and nowhere to love, and they look hopefully to you. Don't turn your back on the poor, because the poor are Christ.

NOVEMBER 8

Let us keep the joy of loving Jesus in our hearts. And let us share that joy with everyone we meet. Passing on joy Is something which is very natural. We have no reason for not being joyful, since Jesus is with us. Jesus is in our hearts. Jesus is in the poor we meet. Jesus is in the smile we give to others, and He is in the smile we receive from others.

NOVEMBER 9

Each one of us is here today because we have been loved by God who created us, and by our parents who cared enough to give us life. Life is the most beautiful gift of God. That is why it is so painful to see what is happening today in so many places around the world; life being deliberately destroyed by war and every type of violence.

NOVEMBER 10

I do not understand why some people are saying that women and men are exactly the same, and are denying the beautiful differences between men and women. All God's gifts are good, but they are not all the same.

NOVEMBER 11

Loving trust and total surrender made Mary say "yes" to the message of the angel. And cheerfulness made her run in haste to serve her cousin Elizabeth. That is so much our life: saying "yes" to Jesus and running in haste to serve Him in the poorest of the poor. Let us keep very close to Our Lady and she will make the same spirit grow in each one of us.

NOVEMBER 12

Never get discouraged. The good you do today, will often be forgotten by tomorrow: Do good anyway. Discouragement doesn't come from God. He is there always at our side encouraging us.

NOVEMBER 13

I can never forget the time when I gave a child to a family and after a few months I heard that the child had become very, very sick. I went to the family and told them: "Give me back that child. I'll take care of the sick child and I'll give you another healthy child." The father look at me and said, "Mother, take my life rather than the child."

NOVEMBER 14

When you are suffering, always remember that the Passion of Christ ends always in the joy of the Resurrection. So, when you feel in your own heart the suffering of Christ, remember the Resurrection has to come. Never let anything so fill you with sorrow as to make you forget the joy of the risen Jesus.

NOVEMBER 15

One day we will each meet the Lord of the Universe. What will we tell Him about the life we lived . . . about how we treated His other children?

NOVEMBER 16

Poverty makes us free. We need to experience the joy of poverty. We choose poverty, we choose not to have things, unlike the poorest of the poor who are forced to be poor. If we do not have something, it is because we choose not to have it. In this, we are free because nothing belongs to us. Our poverty means that we do not have the kind of shoes we may want or the house we may want. We cannot keep things or give anything away or lend anything of value. We have nothing. We own nothing. This is the experience of poverty.

NOVEMBER 17

There is nothing wrong with money. It is what we do with it that makes it a positive or negative influence in our lives. But I have seen it destroy people time and time again. So, be watchful. Nothing will destroy our joy and our connection with God like money.

NOVEMBER 18

"Let your light shine!" Jesus asks this of us all. But to keep a lamp burning, we have to keep putting oil in it. Pray. Pray. Pray.

NOVEMBER 19

All our words will be useless unless they come from within. Words that do not give the light of Christ increase the darkness. Today, more than ever, we need to pray for the light to know the will of God, for the love to accept the will of God, for the courage to do the will of God.

NOVEMBER 20

Be kind to each other. It is better to commit faults with gentleness than to work miracles with unkindness.

NOVEMBER 21

Do we know our poor people? Do we know the poor in our house, in our family? Perhaps they are not hungry for a piece of bread. Perhaps our children, husband, wife, are not hungry for food, or naked, or dispossessed. But are you sure there is no one there who feels unwanted, deprived of affection?

NOVEMBER 22

A life not lived for other is a life not lived.

NOVEMBER 23

I remember that at the beginning of my work I had a very high fever and in that delirious fever I went before Saint Peter. "Go back! There are no slums in Heaven!" he said to me. So I got very angry with him and I said, "Very well! I will fill Heaven with people from the slums and then you will have slums!"

NOVEMBER 24

If you are a joyful, it will shine in your eyes, in your conversation, and in your countenance. You will not be able to hide it because joy overflows.

NOVEMBER 25

Go out into the world today and love the people you meet.

NOVEMBER 26

We can improve our prayer and, flowing from that, our charity toward others. It can be difficult to pray when we don't know how, but we can help ourselves through the use of silence. Souls of prayer are souls of great silence. This silence takes a lot of sacrifice, but if we really want to pray, now is the time to take that step. Without the first step toward silence, we will not be able to reach our goal, which is union with God.

NOVEMBER 27

The future belongs to God. It is in the hands. I find it much easier to accept today, because yesterday is gone and tomorrow has not come. I have only today.

NOVEMBER 28

I am but an instrument. The first time I received an award, I was very surprised. I did not know whether to accept it or not. But I came to the conclusion that I should accept awards in the name of the poorest poor, as a form of homage to them. I think that basically, when awards are given to me, the existence of the poor in the world is being recognized.

NOVEMBER 29

Whoever is dependent on his or her money, or worries about it, is truly a poor person. If that person places his or her money at the service of others, then the person becomes rich, very rich indeed.

NOVEMBER 30

It is easy to love the people far away. It is not always easy to love those close to us. It is easier to give a cup of rice to relieve hunger than to relieve the loneliness and pain of someone unloved in our own home. Bring love into your home for this is where our love for each other must start.

December

DECEMBER 1

The Season of Advent is like springtime in nature, when everything is renewed and so is fresh and healthy. Advent is also meant to do this to us—to refresh us and make us healthy, to be able to receive Jesus in whatever form He may come to us.

DECEMBER 2

Open your hearts to the love of God. He loves you with tenderness, and He will give you not just to give but to share. And when you are praying, ask for courage so that when you give you can give until it hurts. This kind of giving is love in action.

DECEMBER 3

Never worry about numbers. Help one person at a time, and always start with the person nearest you.

DECEMBER 4

Not all of us can do great things, but we can do small things with great love.

DECEMBER 5

Let us touch the dying, the poor, the lonely and the unwanted according to the graces we have received and let us not be ashamed or slow to do the humble work.

DECEMBER 6

God dwells in us. It doesn't matter where you are as long as you are clean of heart. Clean of heart means openness, that complete freedom, that detachment that allows you to love God without hinderance, without obstacles. When sin comes into our lives that is a personal obstacle between us and God. Sin is nothing but slavery.

DECEMBER 7

I can do things you cannot and you can do things I cannot. Together we can do great things.

DECEMBER 8

We need to know when we say yes to God exactly what is in that yes. Yes means "I surrender"—totally, fully, without any counting the cost, without asking, "Is it convenient?" Our yes to God is without any reservations.

DECEMBER 9

I am Albanian by birth. Now I am a citizen of India. I am also a Catholic nun. In my work, I belong to the whole world. But in my heart, I belong to Jesus.

DECEMBER 10

I can understand the greatness of God, but I cannot understand His humility. It becomes so clear in Him being in love with each one of us separately and completely. It is as if there is no one but me in the world. He loves me so much. Each one of us can say this with great conviction.

DECEMBER 11

Come, O blessed Spirit of knowledge and light, and grant that I may perceive the will of the Father. Show me the nothingness of earthly things, that I may realize their vanity and use them only for your glory and my own salvation, looking ever beyond them to you and your eternal reward.

DECEMBER 12

Breathe in me, O Holy Spirit, that my thoughts may all be holy. Act in me, O Holy Spirit, that my work, too, may be holy. Draw my heart, O Holy Spirit, that I love but what is holy. Strengthen me, O Holy Spirit, to defend al that is holy. Guard me then, O Holy Spirit, that I always may be holy. Amen.

DECEMBER 13

Let us not be afraid to be humble, small, helpless, to prove our love for God. The cup of water you give the sick, the way you lift a dying man, the way you feed a baby, the way you teach a dull child, the way you give medicine to someone suffering of leprosy, the joy with which you smile at your own home—all this is God's love in the world today.

DECEMBER 14

It is not a sin to be rich. When it provokes avarice, it becomes a sin. Richness is given by God and it is our duty to divide it with those less favored.

DECEMBER 15

St. Joseph knew, when Mary became pregnant, that this child was not his child. He saw that she was pregnant but didn't know how. If he had gone to the high priest, she would have been stoned to death. Do you see the charity and thoughtfulness of St. Joseph? If we have the same kind of charity and thoughtfulness toward each other, our families will become the abode of the Most High. How beautiful our families will become where there is total thoughtfulness for others.

DECEMBER 16

Holiness grows fast where there is kindness. I have never heard of kind souls going astray. The world is lost for want of sweetness and kindness.

DECEMBER 17

We never base our assistance on the religious beliefs of the needy, but on the need itself. We are not concerned with the religious beliefs of those we help. We only focus on their urgent need for our love and care.

DECEMBER 18

To women: You and I—being women—we have this tremendous gift: the gift of understanding love. I see that so beautifully in the people we serve, in our poor women, who day after day, meet suffering, accept suffering for the sake of their children. I have seen mothers going without so many things, even resorting to begging, so that their children may have what they need.

DECEMBER 19

If we have no peace, it is because we have forgotten that we belong to each other.

DECEMBER 20

One thing I ask of you: Never be afraid of giving. There is a deep joy in giving, since what we receive is much more than what we give.

DECEMBER 21

Life is full of paradoxes. I have found that if you love until it hurts, there can be no more hurt, only more love.

DECEMBER 22

Love has no other message but its own. Every day we try to live out Jesus' love in a very tangible way, in every one of our deeds. If we do any preaching, it is done with deeds, not with words. This is our witness to the Gospel.

DECEMBER 23

In God we live and move and have our being. It is God who gives life to all, who gives power and being to all that exists. But for His sustaining presence, all things would cease to be and fall back into nothingness. Consider that you are in God, surrounded and encompassed by God, swimming in God.

DECEMBER 24

It's not how much we give but how much love we put into giving.

DECEMBER 25

At Christmas, we see Jesus as a little babe—helpless and poor. And he came to love and be loved. How can we love Jesus in the world today?

DECEMBER 26

Am I convinced of God's love for me and mine for Him? This conviction is the sunlight that makes the sap of life rise.

DECEMBER 27

Every time you smile at someone, it is an action of love, a gift to that person, a beautiful thing.

DECEMBER 28

I did not know that our work would grow so fast or go so far. I never doubted that it would live but I didn't think it would be like this. Doubt I never had because I had this conviction that if God blesses it, it will prosper.

DECEMBER 29

There is more hunger in the world for love and appreciation in this world than for food.

DECEMBER 30

The first requirement of prayer is silence. People of prayer are people of silence.

DECEMBER 31

Yesterday is gone. Tomorrow has not yet come. We have only today. Let us begin.